Every Kid's Guide to Living your Best Life

Discover what makes you strong, how to deal with the tough stuff and how to use your "Kid Power" to feel good!

Building Social and Emotional Skills in Elementary-Age Children

YOUR BEST LIFE

Adult-Guided Activities & Games

Sara Jensen-Fritz, MS, Psy.S., Paula Jones-Johnson, BSW, M.Ed., and Thea L. Zitzow, M.Ed.

ISBN: 978-1-59298-393-3

Library of Congress Catalog Number: 2011927011
Printed in the United States of America
First Printing: 2011
15 14 13 12 11   5 4 3 2 1

Marco illustrations by Brian Barber
Book design by Ryan Scheife, Mayfly Design

BEAVER'S POND
PRESS

Beaver's Pond Press, Inc.
7104 Ohms Lane, Suite 101
Edina, MN 55439-2129
(952) 829-8818
www.BeaversPondPress.com

To order, visit www.BeaversPondBooks.com or www.uflipp.com
or call (800) 901-3480. Reseller discounts available.

Disclaimer: This book is not intended to be a replacement for therapeutic treatment by a licensed mental health professional. Adults assisting a child with this book are encouraged to consult a licensed mental-health professional if the child exhibits significant signs of distress. Signs of distress may include, but are not limited to, high anxiety; prevalent sadness; depressed mood and/or dark or depressed drawings or writings; suicidal thoughts or statements; any actions of self-harm; sleep disturbances; changes in eating patterns; persistent, uncontrollable anger; and any other behaviors or symptoms that are of concern.

Table of Contents

To the Child

Things to Know

This book will take you along a trail where you discover how to feel good. You will meet Marco, your new four-legged friend, who knows the way and will show you how to get there!

In this book, you will draw pictures and share your feelings. This will help you feel good even when things are tough.

Marco has many activities for you to do. You will learn fun new ways to:

- Understand your feelings
- Relax
- Think good thoughts
- Feel good about yourself
- Feel good about your life

Here's how you use this book:

First: Find an adult!

Together, you and your adult can share your thoughts and feelings while you do the activities in this book.

Next: Set aside a time to spend with your special adult each week to work in your book.

You feel better about your life when you use the skills in this book. It's important to practice them every day.

For the Adult

Things to Know

Every Kid's Guide to Living Your Best Life is intended to help children develop lifelong, positive coping skills and increase their self-confidence. In our experience:

- Children benefit when **adults assist** them in approaching difficult times positively.
- Children need **social and emotional skills** in order to build a strong foundation for their life success.
- Children who have these skills are more likely to achieve **academic success**.
- Children who are more self-confident are better insulated against many kid challenges, even **bullying**.

This Valuable Resource

- Helps develop the child's **resilience** for life's challenges.
- Fosters **positive thinking**.
- Provides the child with **tools to feel better** during difficult times.
- Incorporates **continued skill practice** to achieve mastery.
- Builds the **adult-child connection**.

Very Important Points:

- Spend at least thirty minutes with the child on a *weekly basis* to work on the activities in the order in which they appear in this book.
- Re-visit the previous lesson right before starting the new lesson.
- **The more times a child practices these lessons and uses them on a daily basis, the more likely it is that the skill will become a habit.**
- Making each skill a **habit** is the key to creating a long-standing positive and resilient attitude in the child.

Please Read:

We realize that some children are faced with more significant challenges or a serious loss. For these circumstances, children may need therapeutic resources.

Meet Marco

Hi, I'm Marco! I like to learn new things and have fun, just like you. I love catching a Frisbee and chasing squirrels. But there are days when no one will throw the Frisbee for me, and the squirrels won't come down from the trees. Then I feel bored or lonely. Everybody has good days and bad days. When I have a bad day I use the ideas in this book to help me feel better.

Follow me down the nature trail and we'll figure out how to feel better and have fun along the way! You'll need the trail map on p. 81. Cut out the map and hang it somewhere so you can see where we've been and where we're going.

Let's get started. You'll draw, play some games, and learn how to feel good.

This book is created by:

_____
(your name)

Age: _____   Grade: _____

My favorite thing to do is: _____

_____

Who Is Important in My Life?

I'd like to meet the people who care about you. We all have someone who cares about us, such as a teacher, neighbor, mom, dad, brother, sister, cousin, or friend. Even pets! Pets care about people, too!

On the lines below, list the names of people and/or pets who care about you and write one special thing about each of them.

Name: _____ What's Special: _____

_____

Name: _____ What's Special: _____

_____

Name: _____ What's Special: _____

_____

Someone cares about ME!

On the following page, draw a picture of you and the important people and/or pets in your life.

 6

Who Cares About Me?

My Life

Did you know that you have stories that you tell yourself about your life? Your story is the way you think about your life and the things that have happened. You may have parts of your life story that you like, and parts that you don't like.
Now, read my story.

On the next page, draw one sad or bad thing that happened to you and that is part of your life story.

Everyone has a life story.

Marco's Story

One happy part of my life story is when I used to run in the park every week with my friend Flipp. We would have lots of fun. We used to run fast and chase each other. One day, I found out that Flipp had to move away. I wondered if I would ever have fun again. That was a sad part of my life story because I knew I would miss my friend.

Flipp

A Sad Part of My Life Story

The Trail to My Best Life Begins Here

Thanks for sharing a little bit about your life. Now it's time to learn some new ways to make your life better. You will learn how to relax, be positive, and be powerful, and how to let go of things that hold you back from living your best life.

On the following page is the start of your new trail. Draw yourself walking next to me.

Start of My Best Life

MY BEST LIFE

The Old Way

Sharing My Story

Draw yourself here walking with Marco.

Talking to Someone I Trust

I can share my sad or bad feelings with someone I trust. Talking to someone I trust makes me feel better. Usually, that person has a way of looking at things in a positive way.

Hanging around positive people I trust can also make me feel good. Positive people are people who:

🐾 Like me.

🐾 Listen to me.

🐾 Encourage me to make healthy choices.

🐾 Believe in me.

🐾 Smile and laugh with me.

🐾 Respect my body.

🐾 Make me feel safe.

🐾 Respect my personal space.

🐾 Help me.

🐾 Say kind things to me.

I can share my feelings with someone I trust.

Draw a picture or write the names of the special people you trust on the next page.

I Can Talk to Someone I Trust

The Feelings Hill

I have many different levels of feelings.

Have you ever stopped to think about all of the different feelings you can have? You can feel happy, sad, scared, or excited. But did you know that there are many *levels* of feelings? You can feel *really* great, or you can feel *pretty* bad.

We can hike the Feelings Hill together on the next page to learn about feeling levels. But first, you need to figure out **how** you are feeling. Once you figure that out, the paw prints will show the level of your feelings. Look on the next page.

In the box on the next page, draw a picture of how you're feeling today.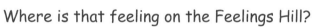

Where is that feeling on the Feelings Hill?

🐾 One paw means you're feeling pretty bad. For example, you really miss someone, or maybe someone teased you.

🐾🐾 Two paws mean you're not feeling okay. For example, you forgot to bring your homework to school.

🐾🐾🐾 Three paws mean you're feeling okay. It's a regular day and all is fine.

🐾🐾🐾🐾 Four paws mean you're feeling pretty good. For example, you got to play your favorite game at recess, or you got a compliment.

🐾🐾🐾🐾🐾 Five paws mean you're feeling great! For example, you felt proud about a school project or you got to go on a field trip!

LET'S PLAY!
Now let's play a game. Cut out the feeling words found on page 65 in the appendix. Read the feeling word (or have someone read it to you) and decide where on the Feelings Hill the feeling belongs. Point to where you think it belongs on the Feelings Hill. It's okay if someone helps you!

Where Am I on the Feelings Hill?

Everyone has feelings.

There are many different levels of feelings.
We can use the paw prints to show our level of feelings.

This is how I am feeling today.

← 🐾 🐾 🐾 🐾 🐾 🐾 Great!

← 🐾 🐾 🐾 🐾 Pretty Good!

← 🐾 🐾 🐾 Okay

← 🐾 🐾 Not So Good

← 🐾 Pretty Bad

Feelings Hill

My Feelings

I can name how I am feeling.

Look at the pictures of me on the next page. The way my face looks shows you how I am feeling.

Choose two of these feelings from the following page. Draw OR write about those feelings below. For example, you could write, "I felt sad when my friend moved away."

DRAW

WRITE

_____

_____

_____

_____

_____

_____

_____

_____

On the next page, color each of the pictures with a color you think matches the feeling. For example, you might color my angry face red or my happy face yellow. Talk about a time you felt each of these feelings.

Marco's Feelings

Angry

Sad

Worried

Excited

Frustrated

Guilty

Scared

Happy

Calm

Changing Heavy Feelings

Most of the time I feel pretty good, but sometimes I don't feel good at all. That's when my feelings get heavy and they tire me out. It feels like work just to do the littlest of things. When I'm sad or mad, my body feels tight or tired. None of this feels good.

The good news is that I can *change* how I feel. The best way to change heavy feelings, like feeling mad or sad or scared, is to stop "holding on" to them. We hold on to feelings when we think about them over and over. You can learn *not* to think about bad feelings over and over again. By practicing the activities in this book or by talking to an adult you trust, you will discover how to let go of the heavy feelings.

Look at my face on the next page. Hanging on to heavy feelings takes work. It's like holding a bag filled with heavy rocks; pretty soon, you get tired. If I can let go of my heavy feelings by thinking about something that makes me feel good, I can feel better! It's like putting down that bag of rocks. I feel better . . . lighter. It's easy to lighten up and feel better; it just takes practice!

Look at the next page. Did you notice that I had to *choose* to put down the heavy things in order to lighten up?

LETTING GO

Letting go of sad or bad feelings isn't easy. If you're not ready to let go of these feelings, that's okay. Find a trusted adult to talk more about them.

When you are ready to let go of the sad and bad stuff, you can try one of these activities. It might help you feel better.

- Write or draw about your sad or bad feelings on a piece of paper. Now, take a deep breath, say good-bye to those feelings, wad it up into a ball, and toss it into a trash can.
- Write or draw about your sad or bad feelings on a piece of paper. Make it into a paper airplane. Take a deep breath, say good-bye to those feelings, and send it into outer space!
- Write or draw about your sad or bad feelings on a balloon. Take a deep breath, say good-bye again, and pop the balloon!

> I feel better when I am able to let go of my heavy feelings.

Sometimes My Feelings Get Heavy

But I Know How to Lighten Up!

Being Powerful

I am powerful when I stand up for myself.

Being powerful means being able to stand up for yourself. When you stand up for yourself, you tell or show someone how you feel without hurting him or her.

Being powerful is not the same as being mean.

Here are three good ways you can stand up for yourself and be powerful when someone says or does something hurtful to you:

1. Say, "No!"

   - Use a firm voice.
   - Stand up tall.
   - Look at the other person's eyes (or at their nose).

   Saying the word "no" makes the other person understand that it is NOT okay to hurt you.

2. Walk away (or ignore the other person).

   Walking away from someone who is being hurtful lets the other person know you don't like what he or she is doing.

3. Ask for help from an adult.

   You don't always have to know the right thing to do. A trusted adult can help you figure out what is best.

Let's **practice . . . practice . . . practice . . .**
It's the only way to get better at it. On the following page, talk over the four examples with the adult helping you with this book. What would you do to be powerful?

Then, draw a picture of you being POWERFUL.

This Is Me Being Powerful!

#1 You are playing with your favorite toy at the park and another kid grabs it out of your hand. To be powerful, you could . . .
- say, "No. That's mine. Please give it back."
- walk toward an adult if you are afraid that the person is going to hurt you.
- talk to a trusted adult about what happened.

#2 Your friend wants you to help her/him cheat on a test. To be powerful, you could . . .
- say, "No. I don't want to."
- ignore your friend.
- ask the teacher if you can sit in a different spot.

#3 Someone puts a hand on your shoulder or touches you in a way you don't like. To be powerful, you could . . .
- say, "No. Stop!"
- walk away.
- ask for help from a trusted adult.

What Would You Do?

On the playground, an older kid pushes you down and says, "You can't play on these monkey bars, only I can play here!! Get out of here!" What would you do? Talk it over with the adult helping you with this book.

Breathing Deeply

Deep breathing helps me feel calm.

Did you know that when you feel stress, your body changes? When you feel stress:

- Your heart may speed up.
- You may breathe faster.
- Your muscles may tense up.
- You may find it hard to think clearly.
- You may feel out of control.

When I get excited, nervous, or just plain stressed out, one of the first things I do is take some deep breaths. It helps me calm down.

Here's what I do. Now you try it!

Sit or lay down comfortably. Breathe in. When you breathe in, your stomach rises. That's because it's filling with air. Now breathe out. When you breathe out, your stomach gently goes back down.

Follow the steps on the next page. Practice this each night before you go to sleep. The next time you feel stressed, you will know how to breathe deeply.

I Can Take 3 Deep Breaths

This Is How I Breathe to Relax.

1. I sit or lay down comfortably.

2. I close my eyes.

3. I place my hand on my stomach.

4. I breathe in deeply through my nose while I count to four. Breathe in 2-3-4. (I can feel my stomach rise.)

5. I breathe out softly through my mouth while I count to four. Breathe out 2-3-4.

6. I do my in/out breathing 3 times.

7. My body feels much more relaxed.

Practice each day and remember:
Breathe in 2–3–4. Breathe out 2-3-4.

Learning to Relax

Another thing I do to feel calm is to tighten and relax my muscles from my toes to my nose. First, I sit or lay down comfortably.

Then I begin an exercise that's called muscle relaxation. **Try it with me!**

Follow the steps on the next page. I breathe in, hold my breath, and tighten certain muscles. I keep my muscles tight and count to five. Then I breathe out and relax my muscles.

Pick one day a week to practice this. I like to do this on Saturday mornings.

Ask an adult to read these eleven steps to you while you practice relaxing.

Relaxing my muscles helps me feel calm.

I Can Relax My Body

First I need to lie down or sit comfortably.
Then I need to slow my breathing.

I will breathe in as I tighten my muscles and breathe out as I relax.

1. I tighten my toes and feet. Hold it . . . hold it . . . hold it . . . now relax.

2. I tighten my calf muscles. Hold it . . . hold it . . . hold it . . . now relax.

3. I tighten my thigh muscles. Hold it . . . hold it . . . hold it . . . now relax.

4. I tighten my tummy muscles. Hold it . . . hold it . . . hold it . . . now relax.

5. I tighten my chest muscles. Hold it . . . hold it . . . hold it . . . now relax.

6. I tighten my fingers and hands. Hold it . . . hold it . . . hold it . . . now relax.

7. I tighten my arms. Hold it . . . hold it . . . hold it . . . now relax.

8. I tighten my shoulders. Hold it . . . hold it . . . hold it . . . now relax.

9. I tighten my neck. Hold it . . . hold it . . . hold it . . . now relax.

10. I tighten my face. Hold it . . . hold it . . . hold it . . . now relax.

11. I tighten my whole body. Hold it . . . hold it . . . hold it . . . now relax.

Imagining a Calm Place

I can also feel calm when I close my eyes and see or think about my favorite quiet place. A calm place is a place where there is not much going on and not much noise. Too much action and noise around you can make your body feel tight instead of relaxed.

Here's a way to practice. Close your eyes and think about what an apple looks like. What color is it? How big is it? Is it the size of your fist, or is it bigger? Now imagine holding the apple and taking a bite. How does it taste? Is it juicy or sour or sweet? You just used your imagination to see and taste the apple.

This time, imagine you are lying outside on a soft towel with your eyes closed. You are barefoot and wearing comfortable clothes. It is a warm, sunny day and you can feel the warm sun on your skin. You feel a gentle breeze and hear the birds singing. Doesn't that feel good?

One of my favorite calm places to imagine is a quiet spot in my yard. I see myself lying in the shade of a big oak tree. I feel a warm breeze on my ears. I can smell the green grass.

What about you? Where is your quiet place?

I can relax by imagining my calm place.

Imagine your quiet place, and then draw a picture of it on the next page.

This Is My Calm Place

Being Kind to Myself

Did you know that it is important to be kind to *yourself*? Being kind to yourself is treating yourself in a way that is good for your mind and body.

Here are some important things that I do to be kind to myself.

🐾🐾🐾🐾🐾 I get plenty of rest.

🐾🐾🐾🐾🐾 I eat healthy foods.

🐾🐾🐾🐾🐾 I go for a walk or a swim, or I chase squirrels.

🐾🐾🐾🐾🐾 I play outside.

On the next page, write or draw about two things that you do to be kind to yourself. Here are some ideas if you need them.

It's important that I be kind to myself.

🐾 Play with my pets

🐾 Play outside

🐾 Read something I enjoy

🐾 Laugh with my friends

🐾 Ride my bike

🐾 Get plenty of sleep

🐾 Relax my body

🐾 Keep my body clean

🐾 Play with my friends

🐾 Eat healthy meals and snacks

🐾 Talk to a friend

I Can Be Kind to Myself

Being Kind to Others

Being kind to **others** is just as important as being kind to yourself. Have you ever noticed that when you are kind to someone, you feel happy inside? Your kindness makes the other person feel good too! Read my story about kindness.

Think of some things that you can do to make others feel better (see some ideas below).

Write or draw about it on the next page. ➡

Ideas:

❀ Compliment someone about an idea they had

❀ Let someone go in front of you in line

❀ Smile

❀ Give up your seat

❀ Ask someone you don't hang out with to play with you

❀ Open a door

❀ Compliment someone about what they are wearing

❀ Be the first to pick up something someone dropped

❀ Be polite to others and say please and thank you

❀ Play with your pet every day

> When I am kind to others, I feel happy.

Marco's Story

Here's what my kind friend Lucky did for me:

Last year I was sad when my friend Flipp moved away. We used to hang out together at the park. I really missed him. The next time I went to the park, I didn't have anyone to play with. Then one day, a friendly dog named Lucky asked me to play. She didn't have to do that, but it sure was kind of her and we had fun together.
Now, when I see other dogs without friends, I ask them to play.

My friend Lucky

I Can Be Kind to Others

Being Grateful

Being grateful means being thankful for someone or something. When you are grateful, you are thankful for things around you or a kindness that someone did for you. Read my story about being grateful.

You probably have people or pets in your life that you are thankful for, too. Maybe you're grateful for a friend who is a good listener, or for a pet who plays with you, or for a teacher who smiles at you every day. I have people like that in my life. I am thankful for *things* too, like my bone, or chew toy, or soft rug.

I think about who or what I am thankful for at least once each day.

In the dog bone shapes on the next page, draw or write about three things that you are grateful for.

> When I think about the things and people I am grateful for, I get a warm, happy feeling inside.

Marco's Story

Here's how I learned about being grateful:

The other day, I couldn't find my favorite chew toy. I looked under my rug, over by the fence, and in my doghouse. It was nowhere to be found! I was frustrated because I wanted that chew toy! Then Lucky came over and helped me find it. She found it in the bushes! Then we played catch with it all afternoon. I am so thankful to have a friend like Lucky!

Lucky

I Can Be Grateful

Tuning In Versus Tuning Out

Sometimes I don't like to think about anything in my life. I like to "tune out." You probably do, too. When I tune out, I stop paying attention to the world around me. I don't have to think about things when I tune out. That's when I don't feel like doing anything. A *little bit* of tuning out is okay, but **too much** tuning out makes me feel tired and cranky. Read my story about tuning out.

"Tuning in" is much better. When I tune in, I'm very quiet and pay close attention to the little things around me. When I go for a walk and listen to the wind in the leaves and feel the green grass under my paws, I'm <u>tuning in</u>. When I spend time outside with my friend, I am <u>tuning in</u>. Tuning in makes me feel really good.

On the next page, you'll see pictures of things that help us tune in or make us tune out.

🐾 Put an X through the things that make us tune out.

🐾 Circle the things that help us tune in.

When I tune in to the world around me, I feel really good.

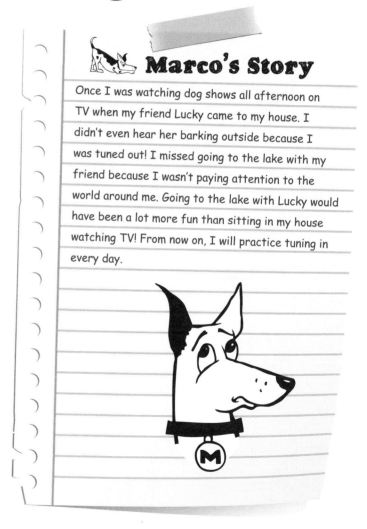

🐾 Marco's Story

Once I was watching dog shows all afternoon on TV when my friend Lucky came to my house. I didn't even hear her barking outside because I was tuned out! I missed going to the lake with my friend because I wasn't paying attention to the world around me. Going to the lake with Lucky would have been a lot more fun than sitting in my house watching TV! From now on, I will practice tuning in every day.

TUNING IN VERSUS TUNING OUT

Remember, tuning out a little is okay,
but tuning out a lot is not.

Practicing Tuning In

Tuning in is good for you because it recharges your body and mind. It works best if you do it every day. But tuning in takes practice. You need to take at least **five minutes** or more every day to practice tuning in. Pretty soon, you will look forward to your tuning in time because it feels so good!

Practice tuning in by following these three simple steps:

1. Turn off the technology (TVs, video games, computers, cell phones, music players, etc.).
2. Take a walk outside.
3. While on your walk, pay attention to your senses. Stay quiet.

   🐾 What do you see? (White puffy clouds in the blue sky?)

   🐾 What do you hear? (A dog barking?)

   🐾 What do you smell? (Blooming flowers?)

   🐾 What do you feel? (Wind blowing through your hair?)

I tune in every day to recharge my body and mind.

In the clouds on the next page, write or draw the things you noticed on your walk!

I Can Tune In

See? Hear? Smell? Feel?

Making Choices

Do you know what a choice is? You have a choice when you have more than one thing to pick from. If someone offers you a piece of fruit, you can choose to take it or choose not to take it. If someone asks if you'd like a banana or an orange, you have a choice!

Sometimes we get to make choices, and sometimes we don't. For example, my family chooses when I eat and when we will go for a walk, but I get to choose whether or not to chase a squirrel or to chew on one of my toys.

Here are some examples of things you can choose and things you cannot choose.

I Can Choose

🐾 What to do for fun

🐾 My friends

🐾 What to read

🐾 To tell the truth

I Cannot Choose

🐾 Whether I go to school

🐾 What I look like

🐾 Where I live

🐾 My family members

On the next page, circle the choices that make you feel the best or add your own.

Making positive choices makes me feel good and is good for me.

Making certain choices, like having certain feelings, can be positive or negative.

Making *positive choices* feels good, and is good for us. For example, eating an apple can be a positive choice because eating apples is good for us. Making a positive choice is great in another way—you feel proud when you make this choice!

Making *negative choices* can sometimes feel good, but negative choices are <u>not</u> good for us. For example, it may feel good at first to eat a big bag of candy, but too much sugar is not good for our bodies.

Feel-Good Choices

I Feel Good When I Choose To:

- talk to someone I trust
- relax my body
- watch a funny movie
- be kind to a friend
- ride a horse
- play with my pet
- go outside to play
- create an art project
- dance
- thank someone
- go sledding

- use deep breathing
- imagine a calm place
- play with my friends
- compliment someone
- listen to music
- help someone
- draw a picture
- call a friend
- go for a walk
- read a book
- be kind to myself

- exercise
- make a fort
- ride a bike
- go to the beach

Having choices feels good.

How about our thoughts?

Do we have choices about how we think?

MARCO'S MAP

The Marco's Map game is found on page 67. Cut apart the game cards found on pages 69 and 71.

DIRECTIONS:

This is a cooperative game. All the players play as a team and use one game piece. The object of the game is to practice the skills in this activity book. Choose any small object as the game piece. Move the marker toward the dog park where Marco's friend Lucky waits. Take turns drawing cards and reading them aloud. Follow the directions on the cards. Continue playing until Marco finds his friend Lucky at the dog park.

Choosing Friends

Choosing your friends is one of the most important choices you will make. Friends are people in our lives whom we can count on. They are there when we need them, just like my friends Lucky and Flipp!

A **GOOD FRIEND** IS SOMEONE WHO:

- listens to you
- is about your same age
- makes good choices
- likes you the way you are
- spends time with you on a regular basis
- makes you laugh
- says nice things about you
- shows respect to others
- takes turns with you
- shares with you
- cares about you

A **NOT-SO-GOOD FRIEND** IS SOMEONE WHO OFTEN:

- talks back to adults
- says mean things to you
- says mean things about you to others
- says they won't be your friend anymore if you play with someone else
- gets in fights with other kids
- doesn't follow the rules
- makes bad choices
- makes you feel uncomfortable

Choosing good friends is important.

Tell your trusted adult about a **good friend** in your life, and why you choose to be friends with him or her.

On the next page, follow the things that a good friend might say to help Marco find Lucky at the end of the maze.

Find your friend by following the good things they would say.

© 2011 UFLIPP • www.uflipp.com • *Every Kid's Guide to Living Your Best Life*

Choosing My Thoughts

Our brains are always thinking. We think about people, places, and things.

Did you know that you have the power to choose <u>what</u> you think and <u>how</u> you think about it?

Believe it or not, a good time to practice choosing your thoughts is during tough times. The next time you have a one-paw or a two-paw day, try to see if you can feel better and make it a three-, four-, or five-paw day! You can do this by **changing the way you think** about what happened. Change a negative thought to a positive thought. It's not always easy to do, but you can do it! Find an adult you trust who can help you practice.

Read each example on the next page. We can choose to have a positive or negative thought about anything.

1. First, imagine a **negative** (sad, mad) thought that you might have about that situation. Practice this for each example.

2. Second, imagine a **positive** (happy) thought that you might have about that situation.

HERE'S HOW YOU DO IT:

"I got a present from a friend that I didn't like."

My bad and negative thought might be:
"I hate this present. My friend never gives me what I want!"
That doesn't feel very good, does it?

My happy and positive thought might be:
"Wow, my friend bought me something. She must really like me! It was so kind of her to buy me something." Now, doesn't that feel better?

I can make my day better by choosing how I think about it.

My friend didn't call me back...

I laughed out loud in class...

I got to go to the movies...

I CAN Choose My Thoughts!

Practice with each example.

I found five dollars on the sidewalk...

I took 2nd place in a race...

I got a present that I didn't like...

My team won the game...

I couldn't buy myself something I wanted...

Choosing Positive Thoughts

Many of my thoughts are valuable: They are keepers and need to be saved. Thoughts like "I am good at playing ball" and "I was proud when I cleaned up my room" are thoughts that are keepers. When I think positively, I am using **positive self-talk**.

Sometimes my thoughts are not very good and need to be thrown away. This is especially true when I start to believe these negative thoughts, even though they are not true. Thoughts like "I'm dumb" or "I'm worthless" should go into the trash. These thoughts do not make me feel good, and I don't want to keep them. When I think negatively, I am using **negative self-talk.**

My Thought Bank Bingo game will help you practice choosing positive self-talk and keep only those thoughts that help you to feel good.

Thought Bank Bingo Game

The Thought Bank Bingo gameboard is found on page 73. Cut apart the game cards found on page 75. Use the blank cards to make your own cards. This game may be played alone or as a cooperative game with others. The object of the game is to get a bingo—5 squares in a row in any direction.

DIRECTIONS:
Put the cards in a cup or bowl. Take one card from the cup and think about how the thought on the card makes you feel. Decide whether that thought is positive and helpful, or negative and not helpful. If it is a positive thought and is positive self-talk, put it in the bank by placing it on top of the picture of a bank on the gameboard. If it is a negative one, put it in the trash by placing it on the picture of a trashcan on the gameboard. If you are playing with someone else, let the next player take a turn picking a card, and decide if the thought is positive or negative. Continue until you get a bingo. Have fun!

Positive thoughts and positive self-talk can help me feel more confident.

I Can Choose Positive Thoughts

I have a choice about what goes into my thought bank!

Positive Thoughts Are Valuable!

I can choose to keep the thoughts that make me feel good.

Negative Thoughts Are Trash!

I can choose to throw away the thoughts that don't make me feel good.

Choosing Positive Self-Talk

Read my story. Then on the following page, write or draw about a time that you could use positive self-talk.

 Marco's Story

Here is a story about how I used positive thinking or positive self-talk to help me be more confident:

Every day when on my nature walk, I would see three geese on my path. These geese would hiss and peck at me and I felt afraid. I said things to myself like, "These geese are going to get me!" and "They won't leave me alone," and "I don't know what to do." These thoughts were negative self-talk. Then I realized that I needed to show the geese that I was strong and confident. So I used positive self-talk and told myself, "I am strong," "I can do this," and "The geese will move when I come by." The next day when I went for a walk, the geese came up to me again. This time I held my head high and barked at them and they moved out of the way! Wow, it really worked! I wasn't mean to them, but I did show them I wasn't going to allow them to peck me anymore.

I Can Choose
Positive Self-Talk

Positive Thoughts Lead to Positive Feelings

Did you know that our thoughts and feelings like to hang out together? Remember there are two kinds of thoughts: positive and negative. **Positive** thoughts, or thoughts that make you feel good, may make you smile, laugh, or relax. **Negative** thoughts, or thoughts that make you feel bad, may make you feel mad, sad, or tense.

You know what kind of thoughts you are thinking by noticing how you are feeling. If you feel bad, you can ask yourself, "What am I thinking?" Once you know your thoughts, you can decide to keep them or throw them away. Then, just like magic, your feelings change! Changing your thoughts takes time and practice, though.

Can you think of a time when your thoughts made you feel happy? How about a time when your thoughts made you feel sad? What were you thinking that made you feel happy or sad?

Show what you are thinking and feeling right now. In the thought bubble, write or draw a picture of what you are thinking. In the heart shape, write or draw about how your thought makes you feel.

Here's an example: "I am thinking about swimming in the lake and I am feeling happy."

I feel powerful when I pay attention to my thoughts and how they make me feel.

HERE'S WHAT I AM THINKING

HERE'S WHAT I AM FEELING

Positive Thoughts Lead to Positive Feelings

Positive Thoughts hang out with Positive Feelings

They are like best friends.

But Remember . . .

If you choose negative thoughts, those thoughts will hang out with negative feelings, and that doesn't feel good.

Stay Positive!

Letting Go of Fear

Sometimes it isn't easy to stay positive, like during the times when you are afraid. Have you ever been so afraid of something that your thoughts turned into negative thoughts? Read my story about letting go of fear.

There are times in your life when you may have to trust that things can get better for you even if you are scared about it at first. You may feel that you can't do something on your own, like go to school on the first day or face a friend who is mad at you. But the more you fight these fears, the stronger the fear becomes.

Try this:

WHAT IS RESISTANCE?

Take a medium-sized basketball, volleyball, or other air-filled ball. Place this ball in a deep tub of water. Notice how it floats without any help. Put both hands on top of the ball. Push the ball down into the water and hold it. What does it feel like? Do you feel the ball pushing up against your hands? Keep holding it under the water until it becomes more difficult to hold on to. This is resistance. Now let go and watch the ball pop up. Think of this ball as your feelings. When you stop resisting your fear, you let go and you make a change and try something new. Then things feel lighter.

Sometimes things get easier when I let go of my fears.

Marco's Story

Here's what happened to me.

One day I was swimming in the river. The water was moving so fast that it pulled me into a culvert that went under the road. I was so scared! The harder I fought the current, the more scared I got. I kept paddling and paddling to try to get out, but that wasn't working. I just couldn't get out; I was resisting or fighting against the river. I had thoughts like, "I'm not strong enough," "This is scary," "What's happening?" and "I don't want to go through this." With each thought, I became more and more afraid. I was so tired! Then I remembered to change my negative thoughts to positive ones. I thought, "I can do this," and "It's going to be okay." I quit resisting and fighting against the river. All of a sudden, I floated through to the other side of the culvert. Finally, I could climb out of the river!

On the next page, write or draw about a time you felt scared and resisted.

I Can Let Go of My Fear

What Scares Me

What I Can Do About It

Change Can Be Okay

I've discovered that lots of things in life change. And you know what? Change doesn't have to be scary.

Here are a few changes that I have had in my life. When I was a puppy, I had short legs and baby teeth; now I have long legs and big teeth. I used to live on a farm with my mom; now I live in a small town. When it gets cold, my fur gets thick; when it gets hot, I shed my fur. Life just changes, that's how it is.

There are changes in your life, too. Each year you get bigger, your body changes, and you change teachers at school. Maybe you have moved to a different house or made new friends.

Sometimes change can make me worry. When I found out I had to move to a small town, I was worried about whether I would fit in with all the other animals in the neighborhood. Then I remembered that **worrying never makes anything better**. So I had to change my thoughts about my new home. I had to stop thinking it was going to be scary. My new thought was, "I can make new friends." I stopped worrying. Now I love my home and have lots of fun with the other dogs on my street.

Change doesn't have to be scary. I can choose better thoughts.

On the next page, name one change that you are worried about right now. Write or draw how that change could turn out okay.

If you can't think of one right now, that's okay. Come back to this page another time.

Change Can Be Okay

A Change I Worry About

How That Change Can
Turn Out Okay

Mistakes Happen

When we make a mistake, we usually feel pretty bad. But guess what? Everybody makes mistakes. And mistakes help us learn. Read my story about a mistake I made.

Things to Remember About Mistakes:

1. It's okay to make mistakes. Everybody does.
2. When you make a mistake, you usually feel bad inside.
3. When your mistake hurts someone, you have to:
   - admit what you did
   - say you are sorry
   - fix it the best you can
4. After you fix it, stop feeling bad and move on.

I can learn from my mistakes.

On the next page is a Fix-It Plan. This can help you work through your mistakes. Think of a mistake that you've made and write about it on the Fix-It Plan. Talk about your answers with an adult.

(Use the Fix-It Plan template on p. 77 as needed.)

Marco's Story

Here's a story about a mistake I made.

One day, Lucky left her favorite chew toy at my house. It was one of those stuffed squirrels with a squeaker in it. I had so much fun chewing it, squeaking it, throwing it up in the air, and catching it. But all of a sudden, it wasn't squeaking anymore and pieces of stuffing had fallen out everywhere. I felt bad because I knew Lucky would be mad at me. I should have been more careful with her toy. I made a mistake and wished I could undo it.

Later, when Lucky came over, I didn't know what to do. My first thoughts were, "I can hide the toy and she'll never find it," or "Maybe I can tell Lucky that the big dog next door took it and ruined it!" But I knew if I didn't tell her the truth, I would feel much worse.

I had to be honest and tell Lucky what I did. I told her what really happened and that it was all my fault. After telling Lucky I was sorry, I gave her one of my favorite toys. That was tough, but I knew it was the right thing to do. Lucky was glad I told her.

My Fix-It Plan

1. This is what happened.

   _____

   _____

   _____

2. Here is something I can do to fix it.

   _____

   _____

   _____

3. Here is one thing I can do differently next time.

   _____

   _____

   _____

Power Statements

Power statements can help you believe in yourself. They are statements you say to yourself to help build self-confidence and feel good about who you are. Power statements begin with an "I" and are about something positive you want to believe about yourself. They work best when you say them out loud to yourself every day.

Power statements help me believe in myself.

My power statement is "I am a good friend," so my picture shows my friend playing with me.

Power-Up Practice:

- Cut out a power statement from the list on p. 79 in the appendix.
- Tape it on your bathroom mirror.
- Stand in front of the mirror.
- Say the power statement out loud.
- Do this each day until you really believe it.

On the following page, write a power statement and choose a time you will practice it each day. Draw a picture of how your Power Statement looks when you truly believe it.

My Power Statement

My Power Statement is: _____

_____

_____

I will say it every day at: _____

This is what my Power Statement looks like (draw below).

My Positive Feelings Are Magnets for Good Things

> Positive thoughts help me reach my goals.

When you choose positive thoughts, you feel good. Did you know that when you feel good, you often choose to do positive things to match that feeling? And did you know that those positive actions will then bring good things into your life? Well, they will! When you think a positive thought and do a positive action, you are like a big magnet that attracts other positive things into your life.

Follow the arrows in the example below to see how this works.

"I can learn to play catch." (thought)   **I practice catching every day. (action)**   *Leads to*

Leads to   **I feel confident! (feeling)**   *Leads to*

I become a better catcher! (Even better feeling)

The same can happen for you! When you *think* positive, *feel* positive, and *act* in a positive way, you will feel great!

 On the following page there are three boxes. In the first box, **draw or describe one of your goals**. Some examples of goals are: you want to go to summer camp, or be a better baseball player, or maybe you want to have a new bike.

 In the middle box, **draw or describe one positive thought** that will help you reach your goal. For example, if your goal is to have a new bike, a positive thought might be, "I can find ways to earn money."

 In the last box, **draw or describe at least one thing you need to do to reach your goal**. For example, "To earn extra money for my new bike, I will have a lemonade stand."

Positive Feelings Lead to Good Things

When you feel good you attract good things.

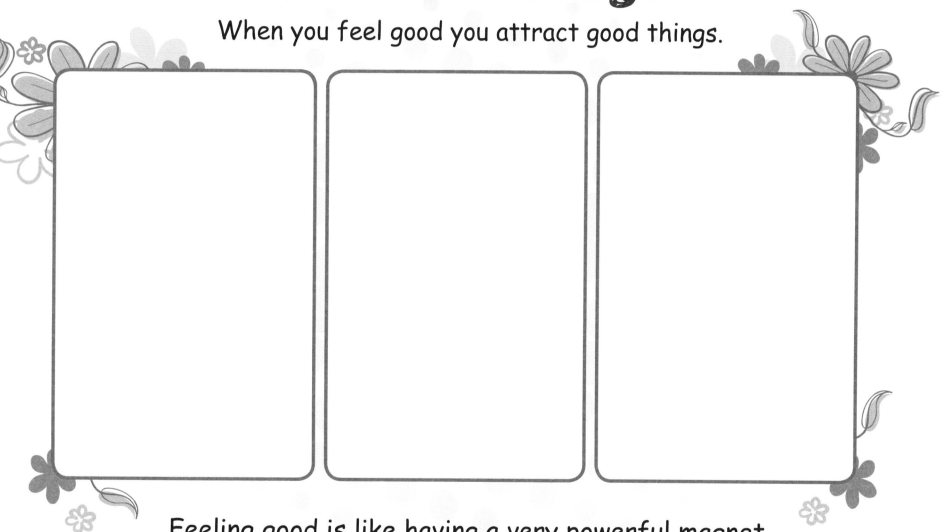

Feeling good is like having a very powerful magnet that brings good things to you.

Writing My Story

Now that you know how to choose positive thoughts, it's time to use those good thoughts to write a story about **YOU**.

When you think about your story, remember these four important facts that are true for everybody.

➡ **Know** that you are *special*. No one else is exactly like you. No one else has your smile or can do things exactly the way you do. That's pretty cool, huh?

➡ **Know** there is a reason you were born. You **bring joy** to others every day. Without you, everyone else's story would be different.

➡ **Know** that the not-so-good parts of your life story can help you grow **stronger**. You made it through the tough stuff. Congratulations!

➡ **Know** that you are always in charge of the way you *think* about your life story. You can think about the bad things and feel bad, or think about the good things and feel good.

> I am special, no matter what has happened in my life.

With help from an adult, fill in the blanks of your story on the next page. Use the ideas below if you need them.

For being me:

I am special because:

*I have nice eyes   *I have a funny laugh   *I have a big smile

*I have a twitchy nose   *I have a sprinkling of freckles   *I have a strong voice

*I can sing like a bird   *I can make funny faces   *I have great ideas

*I am creative   *I can draw   *I can build things

For helping others:

I am special because:

*My laugh makes others smile   *I give great hugs that make others feel better

*I love my pets and take care of them   *I listen to others when they need to talk

*I comfort my friends   *I take turns with my friends

*I share my things   *I tell others what I like about them

I Can Write My Story

I am _____ and I was born for a special reason.
(name)

I am special for **being me** because _____

_____.

I am also special because I **help others** by _____

_____.

Even though I have had challenges in my life, I have grown stronger from the tough stuff.

I can think about the **good things** in my life, like:

1. _____

2. _____

3. _____

I feel better when I think about the good things!

Happy Trails

**Thanks for following me on the trail.
I had fun and hope you did, too!**

Find My Daily Reminder in the Appendix.
Color it then hang it where you can see it every day.
Remember to practice what you've learned.

Remember, **YOU** have the power to live your best life! It only takes **PRACTICE**.

Appendix

Feeling Words

Happy	EXCITED	Sad	Proud	Grumpy
Mad	Frustrated	Guilty	Confident	Embarrassed
Worried	Scared	SURPRISED	Joyful	Nervous

65

Marco's Map Game

Start

Finish

Marco's Map Game Cards

A Cooperative Team Game

I resisted a change in my life. Go back 3 spaces. 	I am grateful for _____ (person). Walk ahead 3 spaces 	I am grateful for _____ (thing). Walk ahead 3 spaces. 	I made someone smile. Walk ahead 2 spaces. 	I tuned in and took a walk outside. Walk ahead 2 spaces. 
I did my homework. Walk ahead 3 spaces. 	I helped my friend. Walk ahead 2 spaces. 	I tuned out and played video games all day. Go back 2 spaces. 	I played outside. Walk ahead 2 spaces. 	I finished my chores. Walk ahead 3 spaces. 
I did not do my chores. Go back 1 space. 	I took 3 deep breaths when I was stressed. Walk forward 3 spaces. 	I told myself "I can do it!" when I felt unsure. Walk forward 2 spaces. 	I built a fort. Walk ahead 2 spaces. 	I went to bed on time. Walk ahead 3 spaces. 

Marco's Map Game Cards

A Cooperative Team Game

I told a lie. Go back 1 space. 	I was nice to someone. Walk forward 3 spaces.	I teased someone. Go back 1 space.	I shared my feelings with someone I trust. Walk forward 3 spaces.	I imagined a calm place when I was stressed. Walk forward 3 spaces.
I was respectful toward others. Walk forward 3 spaces. 	I was disrespectful to an adult. Go back 1 space. 	I fought with my brother or sister. Go back 1 space. 	I argued with my teacher. Go back 1 space. 	I told myself I was worthless. Go back 2 spaces. 
I asked for help. Walk forward 3 spaces. 	I hurt someone's feelings on purpose. Go back 1 space. 	I apologized for something I did wrong. Walk ahead 3 spaces. 	I tuned out and watched TV all day. Go back 2 spaces.	I tuned in and went for a bike ride. Walk ahead 3 spaces. 

Thought Bank Bingo Gameboard

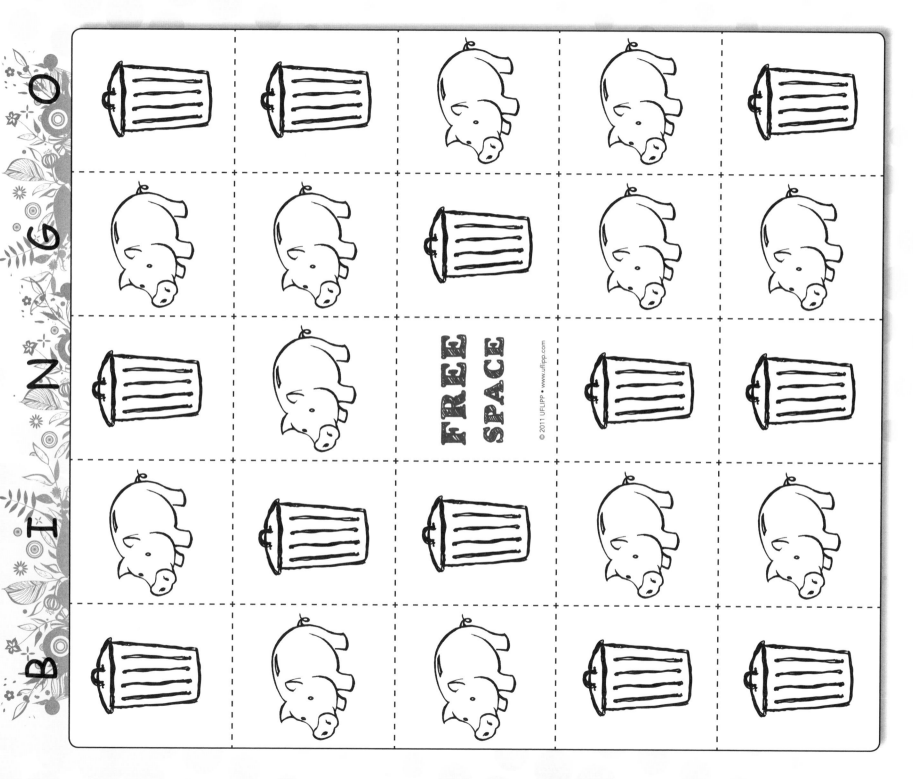

B I N G O

FREE SPACE

© 2011 UFLIPP • www.uflipp.com

Thought Bank Bingo Cards
A Cooperative Team Game

I hate my friend.	Challenges make me stronger.	I can learn.	I'm horrible at math.	I'm fat.	I keep trying.
I went for a walk.	I like to play with my pet.	I never get to do fun things.	I'm stupid.	I'm healthy.	I'm a good person.
I think she's mean.	I like myself.	Things will turn out okay.	I hate myself.	Somebody loves me.	I hate school.
I have friends.	I can do it.	That's too hard for me.	I'm bad.	I'm helpful.	I'm afraid I'm not good enough.
No one likes me.	I get things done.	I do my work.	I like school.	I can't do anything right.	No one understands me.
I never get my way.	I don't have any friends.	People like me.			

My Fix-It Plan

1. This is what happened.

_____

_____

_____

2. Here is something I can do to fix it.

_____

_____

_____

3. Here is one thing I can do differently next time.

_____

_____

_____

You have permission to copy this Fix-It Plan as needed.

Power Statements

I am safe in my world.	I am loved.	I am brave.
I am perfect exactly as I am.	I am healthy and filled with energy.	I am worth loving.
I am a healthy person.	I stay positive.	I am willing to change.
I accept all parts of myself.	I love my family.	I have choices.
I like being me.	I am kind to others.	I care about others.
I am creative.	I can solve problems in my life.	I am okay.
I am willing to forgive.	I let go of my fears.	I am calm and relaxed.
I speak and think positively.	I am strong.	I have good relationships.
I love myself exactly as I am.	I am good enough.	I am a good friend.
I have the power to make changes.	I can make my life better.	I have a good life.

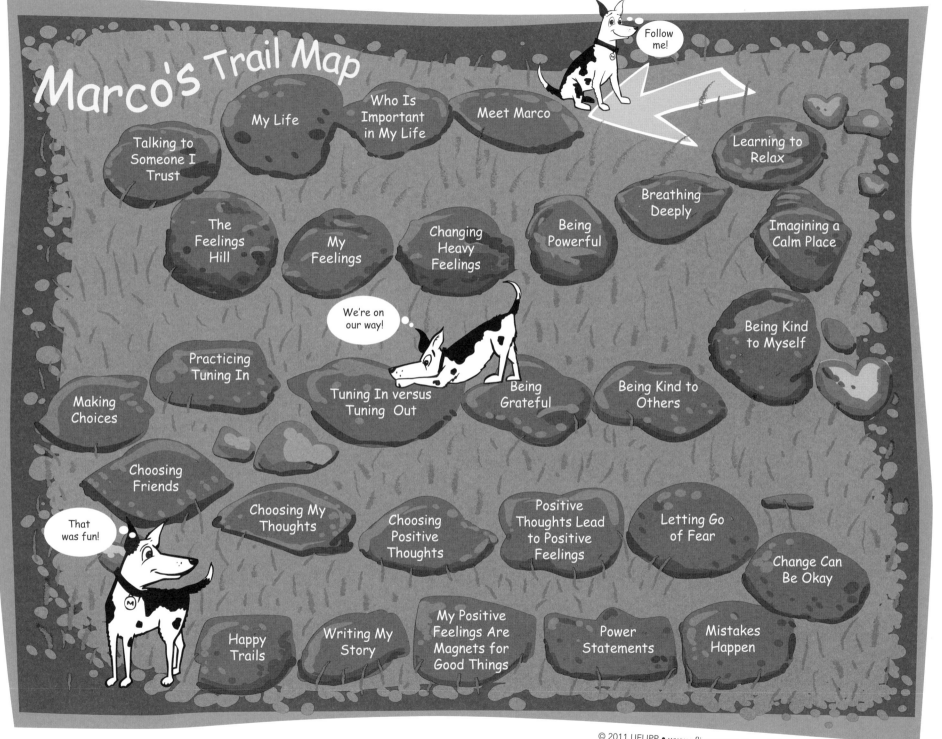

About Marco

Marco was born January 11, 2009, in a small barn near Hitterdahl, Minnesota. Marco's mom is an Australian Shepherd and his dad is a Black Lab. He and the other puppies were brought to a kennel so that someone could find homes for them. Marco stayed until he was discovered by his owner.

WHERE'S MARCO NOW?
Marco lives on a small hobby farm in Minnesota where he hangs out with four horses, two older dogs, two indoor cats, and one barn cat. He likes his big family and lots of space to play outside.

WHAT MAKES MARCO HAPPY?
Marco's favorite thing in life is playing Frisbee. When you say, "Frisbee!" he gets as excited as you would if it were your birthday! So, Marco feels like it is his birthday every day! His other favorite things include chasing squirrels, herding the horses, going for walks, and catching the ball over and over and over again. Marco is very speedy and can catch a fast ball, a curve ball, or even a bouncy ball.

Oh, one more thing…Marco loves it when you say, "Good boy, Marco!" and lightly rub his ears.

About Us

About UFLIPP

Today's kids are faced with real-world stress and pressures without the maturity and experience to adapt. However, this doesn't mean they can't learn to relax, understand what they're feeling, and love themselves and life. It is our hope that *Every Kid's Guide to Living Your Best Life* will provide children with the opportunity to learn social and emotional skills that create a foundation for resilience. Our passion is helping children live successful and happy lives!

UFLIPP books and products are designed to assist children in building the **skills of resilience** while establishing a **positive connection** between the adult and child.

About the Authors:

Our education and experience working with children in individual and group settings collectively spans 60 years, including areas of expertise in clinical psychology, applied behavioral analysis, school psychology, counseling, social work, special education, and speech/language pathology.

First UFLIPP book:

You and Your Military Hero

This book honors the deployed loved one while teaching military children positive thinking skills.

You can find all of UFLIPP books and products at www.uflipp.com.